LETTERS TO A YOUNG DOUBTER

LETTERS

TO A

YOUNG

DOUBTER

WILLIAM SLOANE COFFIN

Westminster John Knox Press
LOUISVILLE • LONDON

Book design by Teri Vinson
Cover design by designpointinc.com

First edition
Published by Westminster John Knox Press
Louisville, Kentucky

This book is printed on acid-free paper that meets the
American National Standards Institute Z39.48 standard. ∞

PRINTED IN THE UNITED STATES OF AMERICA

07 08 09 10 11 12 13 14 – 11 10 9 8 7 6 5 4

Library of Congress Cataloging-in-Publication Data is on
file at the Library of Congress, Washington, D.C.

ISBN: 978- 0-664-22929-0

DEDICATION

This book is dedicated to my older brother, Ned, and his wife, Vi; to my younger sister, Margot, and her husband, Frank;

and

to all eighteen-year-olds eager to pledge allegiance "to the earth, and to the flora and fauna and human life that it supports; one planet indivisible, with clean air, soil and water, with liberty, justice and peace for all."

ACKNOWLEDGMENTS

This book owes much to the suggestions and assistance of Stephanie Egnotovich, Marjorie Stewart, John Maguire, Wil and Jill Tidman, and (always) to Randy Wilson Coffin.

PREFACE

In 1903, an aspiring young poet named Franz Xavier Kappus began what turned into a five-year correspondence with the great and unique German poet Rainer Maria Rilke. Some twenty years later Rilke's letters were published alone in a volume entitled *Letters to a Young Poet.*

Recently I reread these letters and was once again taken by Rilke's advice "to be patient towards all that is unsolved in your heart and to try to love the questions themselves." Then gradually, Rilke suggests, "you will live into the answers."

"Love the questions and live into the answers." That struck me as a wonderfully wise way to view a growing and evolving life. As for eighteen years I was university chaplain at Yale, it occurred to me that I might write a similar (more modest) volume entitled *Letters to a Young Doubter.* I pictured a bright college student and an exchange of letters lasting over the nine months of an academic year. We would have much to talk about, this imagined friend and I: problems of faith, the difficulties of personal life, and the ever more confusing and complex problems in today's world, seemingly more intent on fighting God's will, than doing God's will.

In my experience, a religious faith despite doubts is far stronger than one without doubts. I suspect that no one so reveals an absence of faith as a dogmatist.

WILLIAM SLOANE COFFIN
Strafford, Vermont
August 2004

little too much relish. But don't be anxious about your newfound doubts. Doubts move you forward not backward, just as long as you doubt out of love of the truth, not out of some pathological need to doubt. As Emily Dickinson wrote, "The unknown is the mind's greatest need, and for it no one thinks to thank God."

In searching for new truths, however, don't insist on absolute intellectual certainty. As Pascal said famously, "*Le coeur a ses raisons que la raison ne connaît point.*" (Go translate.) You are a fine violinist, so you know that the truths of music are apprehended at a much deeper level than they are comprehended. Feelings being treacherous, the mind must play a corrective role, but no seeker of truth should ignore what Leonard Bernstein wrote about Beethoven: "He broke all the rules and turned out pieces of breathtaking rightness." The same, of course, could be said of great painters and poets, and, as a matter of fact, that's pretty much the way I feel about God.

If you are of a mind to do so, keep me posted on your progress. Meantime my affectionate wishes accompany you as well as my total confidence in your bright collegiate future.

Love,

Bill

PS: Why am I giving you one more assignment when you have too many already? Pascal wrote, "The heart has its reasons of which the mind knows nothing."

Dear Tom,

Thanks for the second letter and for the proposal of a continuing correspondence. For me it is
a rejuvenating idea, so let's try it, but let's also be
clear about the ground rules: I won't treat you as
if eighteen were too young, and you won't treat
me as if eighty were too old. Actually my part of
the bargain may be easier. St. Benedict said, "God

often shows what is better to the younger." You, on the other hand, may think wisdom comes with age. Believe me, Tom, age often comes alone.

You are right to insist that doubts are quite different in kind. The ones I had in mind in my last letter didn't so much concern knowledge, which is primarily a cerebral affair; they concerned wisdom—a matter of heart, mind, and soul, all pulling together.

Allow me to change your doubts into "questions." Tolstoy once suggested that certain questions are put to humanity not so much that we should answer them but that we should spend a lifetime wrestling with them. I don't recall Tolstoy listing any such questions, so here's one of my own: "Who tells you who you are?"

Let me illustrate. When I was chaplain at Yale, it was natural that seniors bound for graduate school should come to me for letters of recommendation. (They didn't realize that education kills by degrees!) To such highfalutin schools as the Harvard Law School or the Columbia Medical School, I often said, "In all likelihood, this candidate will be in the bottom quarter of your class. But surely you will agree with me that the bottom quarter should be as carefully selected as the top. And for what should you be looking in the bottom quarter if not a candidate who will seek the common good rather than personal gain; who will strive to be valuable rather than successful, and to make a difference, not money? As this candidate embodies these virtues, I consider him failed. Such is the power of higher education to tell you who you are!

So, dear Tom, my question for you today is "Who tells you who you are?" Love the question, as German poet Rilke would say, and live into the answer. You have a lifetime. But start now.

Love,

Bill

neither scholarship nor athletics, money nor power, are bad in themselves; quite the contrary, as long as they remain in a penultimate position. It's when they become the ultimate things in our lives, when they tell us who we are, that they become what the ancient Hebrews called "idols."

When people stop believing in God, the trouble is not that they thereafter believe in nothing, but that they believe in anything. And closer observation tells you more: only the rich idolize money, or the poor who think, "If I were only rich, I'd be someone." Only Americans idolize America. No American idolizes France unless he speaks very good French. In other words, idolatry is worship of the self projected into objective form. Or let's put it this way: a truly religious person has infinite love only for the infinite, whereas an idolator has infinite love for something finite. Psalm 115 talks of idols of silver and gold, "the work of human hands." And then goes on to say of these figures:

They have mouths, but do not speak;
eyes, but do not see.
They have ears, but do not hear;
noses, but do not smell.
They have hands, but do not feel;
feet, but do not walk . . .

Then comes the stunning line:

Those who make them are like them;
so are all who trust in them.

Talk about dehumanization!

You neglected to mention in your list of eligible idols one important possibility. Some people need their failures to tell them who they are. The way these people treasure their mistakes, you'd think they were the holiest things in their lives. Not a few of them think themselves religious, but in fact they have only enough religion to make themselves miserable. And they're also self-centered, as guilt is the last stronghold of pride. Guilt represents your opinion of yourself, while forgiveness represents the opinion of someone else, or of God. Those who treasure their sins are too proud to let someone else do for them what they cannot do for themselves. (Sometimes it's more blessed to receive than to give. At least it takes more humility.)

If you are of a mind to do so, I'd be curious to know what you think it would be like to have God tell you who you are.

With continued gratitude for your letters,

Love,

Bill

PS: Too easily, I think, I have let ambition off the hook. St. Augustine said, "Anybody who needs more than God as his witness is too ambitious."

IV

Dear Tom,

You're right, I shouldn't have pressed you concerning your feelings about God. We learn more when we don't try to understand too soon. To quote once again the belle of Amherst, Emily Dickinson: "The Truth must dazzle gradually,/or every man be blind."

It may, however, be worthwhile to say a word

about what I have found to be a common phenomenon in American universities today. Professors judge poetry, novels, art, and music by their very best works. Why then do so many judge religion by the worst examples of it? I used to ask professors, "Tell me about the God you don't believe in." I knew that 99 chances out of 100 I wouldn't believe in their kind of God either.

I remember a small faculty gathering of good friends, wonderful people. With genuine curiosity I asked them, "Isn't the existence of God a lively question?" Answered a political scientist: "Bill, it's not even a question, let alone a lively one."

As you can imagine, I couldn't let that statement fly by, so I said, "I can understand doubting the quality of the bread, but I can't see kidding yourself that you're not hungry—unless, of course, your soul has so shriveled up that you have no more appetite left for the great mysteries of life, especially the Mysterium Tremendum. And that's what I think has happened to so many of you, and why"—I smiled—"some of you are pretty boring."

At that point, two wives who had come along started to clap.

Needless to say, their husbands were taken aback and a lively discussion ensued. As I remember, we agreed at least that good thinking must include, not exclude, the imagination. Not all of them, however, concurred with Einstein's contention that imagination is more important than knowledge.

I tell you this story because the so-called "pursuit of truth" properly implies that there is a gap between ourselves and the truth. But what's hidden and who's being evasive? Is it we or the truth? Maybe it's we who evade truth's quest for us. In any event, it's clear that while blind belief of any religious stripe is bad for us, the nation, and the world, the answer to blind belief is not blind unbelief.

It's a cold November day here, but the memory lingers on of Vermont's finest hour. A month ago Moses would not have known at what bush to turn aside!

With warm and affectionate greetings,

Bill

V

Dear Tom,

Thanks for your ever-rejuvenating letters.
Among other good things, they remind me of all
the undergraduates I knew and loved, many now
crowding sixty, even seventy. Some have aged
like vintage wine, heeding Albert Camus's wisdom: "To grow old is to pass from passion to
compassion." A few, however, looking back on

the springtime of their lives, say, "Ah, those were the days"—and the worst of it is, they're right! It was not the days, I suspect, but they who used to be better. May you escape their ranks.

You're smart to decide you have to unlearn as well as learn, to clear away the weeds and thickets in order to see more clearly various paths ahead. And you're absolutely right in recognizing that religion seems to bring out the worst as well as the best in people. You ask for a comment.

I think self-righteousness is the bane of human relations, of all of them—interpersonal, international, and interfaith. I'm sure it was self-righteousness that prompted Pascal to say, "Human beings never do evil so cheerfully as when they do it from religious conviction." Self-righteousness blocks our capacity for self-criticism, destroys humility, and undermines the sense of oneness that should bind us all.

Self-righteousness inspired the Christian Crusades against Muslims and, centuries later, the Easter pogroms of Eastern Europe, the sermon-induced slaughter of Jews after the morning celebration of the resurrected rabbi.

Today this same self-righteousness encourages some American Christians to cheer President Bush's messianic militarism, a divinely ordained form of cleansing violence, and all in the name of a Jesus Christ who is the mirror opposite of the Jesus of the four Gospels.

Self-righteousness makes believers of all

faiths doctrinaire, dogmatic, and mindlessly militant. And, of course, it can just as easily do the same for nonbelievers.

What is heartening about university life is its professed commitment to an open mind. But the virtue of a mind open at one end can become the vice of a mind open at both. So much of what passes at universities for tolerance looks a lot like abdication. A fine rabbi, the late Leo Baeck, once asked, "Which is worse, the intolerance that commits outrages or the indifference that observes outrages with an undisturbed conscience?"

Over the years I have been convinced that the more important question is not who believes in God, but in whom does God believe. Rather than claim God for our side, it's better to wonder whether we are on God's side. Faith is being grasped by the power of love, and there are many atheists with "believing" hearts, the part of us that *should* be religious if you can offer only one.

I'll await, as I always do, your next letter. Meantime, amid intellectual thickets and weeds, do as the British say at cricket games: "Press on regardless."

Cheers,

Bill

VI

Dear Tom,

I'm quickly realizing how much more you know than I did, way back then.

Of course at eighteen I was about to join the infantry and World War II to learn some other things. Probably the most important was never to have an experience and miss the meaning.

But back to your letter. You say that self-righteousness connotes pride, which hardly takes care of self-deprecation. You ask, "Are small egos any less self-referential than large egos?" I was also impressed that from your churchgoing days you recalled, "We have left undone those things which we ought to have done, and we have done those things which we ought not to have done."

That line covered the waterfront, didn't it?

I'm not surprised that in her youth, as your mother told you, she lacked self-confidence. It's an old story. Shakespeare saw the consequences:

Our doubts are traitors
And make us lose the good we oft might win
By fearing to attempt.

Around the time your mother went to college, people were familiar with what Eleanor Roosevelt (FDR's widow) wrote another young woman, also in college, "Remember, dear, it takes two to feel inferior." It was an appropriate reminder from a truly liberated woman. But the pressures at the time against women's liberation were enormous. When I was young, women taught in grammar and high schools, but rarely at universities. They were nurses yet hardly ever doctors. They were secretaries but seldom law partners; fewer yet were clergy, and I can't remember a single woman cop, firefighter, or professional athlete. In short, beyond being racist and homophobic, society in my youth was exceedingly sexist.

As I grew older, I loved women; they charmed me, and I may even have charmed a few of them, but rarely did I consider women's lives as important as those of men. That, of course, is the essence of male chauvinism, and the viciousness of pride that is not accidentally but essentially competitive.

I must have been middle-aged before I came to see a feminist as a woman who refuses to be a masochist. I also was persuaded that the woman most in need of liberation was the woman in every man just as the man most in need of liberation was the man in every woman. Since then I've considered myself at best a recovering chauvinist.

It's good that, surmounting her doubts, your mother went on to medical school and that becoming a doctor gave her the self-assurance that should never have been taken from her. If male chauvinism is less of a problem in your generation than it was in mine, let's give women all the credit; they refused to live the lie!

A final thought. While distinct, pride and self-deprecation may not be that far apart. You remember the Greek mythological figure Narcissus, the man by a pool who kept staring at his reflection in the water. Someone once suggested that he was responding to a sense of unworthiness with defiance.

How's that for a definition of narcissism?

Yours happily in continuing dialogue,

Bill

VII

Dear Tom,

As your counter to narcissism you offer humility defined as objectivity—being objective about your strengths and shortcomings. I like that. The only drawback is the one noted by Thoreau: a man can no more see himself than he can look backward without turning around.

And now you ask, "How did you get religious?" (Long day ahead!)

I will tell you how I became a Christian. By similar paths I could as easily have become a Jew or Muslim. I say this because the instinct to love God and neighbor is equally at the heart of Islam and Judaism as well as Christianity. All three faiths are different, but not different up or different down—just different with a lot to learn from one another.

I'm tempted to say I lost the battle to be anything but religious. The first reason was four years in the military during and right after World War II. The brutalities I witnessed made short shrift of my boyhood innocence, of any naive idealism I might have had. In Europe I found out that Nazis could spend their days gassing Jews and their evenings listening to Beethoven's Razumovsky quartets; the heroic advances of the Soviet armies were accompanied by pillage and rape; and I heard more than one Frenchwoman confess, "I hate to say this, but it felt safer when the Germans were here."

I didn't grieve my lost innocence. In the sullied stream of human life, innocence is not an option. Endearing in kids, it's a lethal form of denial in adults. As Graham Greene was to write in his '50's novel *The Quiet American*, innocence should wander the world wearing a leper's bell.

So I came to college in the fall of '47 primed with the right questions, which is important because few things are more irrelevant than answers to unasked questions. I wanted to know, How can humanity be so inhuman? Conversely, Why does a soldier fall on the grenade there is no time to throw back?

(Among my other questions there was none about joining Zeta Zeta Zeta. I may sound old and crabby, Tom, but I have long viewed fraternities as monuments to irrelevance. To put a prejudiced person in a fraternity and expect him to become broad-minded is about as realistic as putting a wino in a wine cellar and expecting him to lay off the bottle.)

Once in college I searched hard for answers. I read the French existentialists—"crisis thinkers"—Jean-Paul Sartre, Simone de Beauvoir, André Malraux, and especially Albert Camus, all professed atheists. Also I steeped myself in Reinhold and Richard Niebuhr, and Paul Tillich, all profound theologians. My mind went toward the atheists, but my heart was pulled toward the theologians. Both had a tragic sense of life, both knew what hell was all about, but in the depths of it the theologians found a heaven that made more sense out of everything, much as light gives meaning to darkness.

Sensing a troubled soul, a small band of Christian students came to convert me. But their answers seemed too pat; their submission to God, too ready. It occurred to me that as with parents so with God; too easy a submission is but a facade for repressed rebellion. Besides, they didn't look redeemed!

Actually I was right about their repressed rebellion. When I told them it was time for us to part company, their leader said with a sweetness that thinly veiled his hostility, "Well, Bill, you'll always be on our prayer list." I couldn't help but ask, "And how does your prayer list differ from your shit list?"

More helpful was singing in the University Chapel choir, two anthems every Sunday. And I listened to what was said in the sermons and prayers. I remember well the first Sunday I really heard the Episcopal invocation that begins, "Almighty God, unto whom all hearts are open, all desires known, and from whom no secrets are hid. . . ." Who in the world, I wondered, would want to believe in a God that saw that much?

Then the prayer goes on: "Cleanse the thoughts of our hearts by the inspiration of thy Holy Spirit. . . ." Why the thoughts of our hearts and not our minds?

For a good week, I worried that question. Then I realized that while the heart may have its reasons about which the mind knows nothing (you remember Pascal?), the mind has hardly any thoughts that are not in some way connected to the heart. If you have a heart of stone, you can dissect bugs but you can't understand, let alone enter deeply into, human relations. But a heart full of love has a limbering effect on the mind. Faith is no substitute for thinking; it should help make good thinking possible. In fact, love calls for the utmost in clear-sightedness, all of which I later found out was well understood by Roman Catholics, who called prudence the first of the four cardinal virtues. *Prudentia* really means "damn good thinking."

The upshot of all this puzzling was positive. I started, à la Rilke, "to love the questions" and "to live into the answers," waiting patiently for the disclosure of more. Following the advice of Alcoholics Anonymous, I decided to commit as much of myself as I could to as much of God as I believed in. That struck me as an honest way of proceeding.

Sunday by Sunday Jesus became more and more real to me. I loved the way he relied on narrative and example rather than on precept and principle. What he said, what he did, struck me as words and deeds of "breathtaking rightness." In the sullied and bloody stream of life, not innocence but holiness was the option he offered. And holiness didn't mean being upright (read "uptight") but rather knowing such a joy that could absorb all sorrow, a hope that could surmount despair, and knowing that caring is the greatest thing in life (read tough-minded unsentimental love).

But while I could converse with Jesus, I still couldn't pray to God, mostly I think, because in a world of pain I simply couldn't believe in a God immune from it.

One Sunday, however, I was brought up short. If what was so admirable about Jesus was the fact that from the outer periphery to his inner core, creed and deed were one, who would know more about the existence of God—Jesus or I, myself? It was a little hard to say, "Naturally, I do."

Gradually the dazzling truth dawned on me—although it was not high noon for a few more years. Finally in seminary I saw that Jesus was both a mirror to humanity and a window to divinity, the modest amount given to mortal eyes to see. God was not confined to Jesus, but, to Christians at least, essentially defined by Jesus. When we see Jesus scorning the powerful, empowering the weak, healing the hurt, always returning good for evil, we are seeing transparently the power of God at work. So as regards the divinity of Christ, what's finally important is less that Christ be Godlike but more that God is Christlike. That means that in a world of pain

God is anything but immune from it. "Behold, he who keeps Israel will neither slumber nor sleep." Maybe it's the pain and not the peace of God that "passes all understanding." And to think that the magnitude of human malpractice notwithstanding, there is more mercy in God than sin in us. How have we confidence in that knowledge? "Through Jesus Christ our Lord," the proper way to end all Christian prayers.

Now my question to you, dear Tom, is, "Do you think God is too hard to believe in, or too good to believe in, we being strangers to such goodness?"

Love the question!

Bill

PS: This was a long letter. Your fault!

VIII

Dear Tom,

I get the impression that some of your questions have been addressed by your roommates to you and then you want me to answer them. That's fine, but be sure always to ask them, "Is this question personal or merely academic?" Too many college students are better able to tell you what's on anybody else's mind than on their own. Rarely are they pressed for their own deep beliefs.

Your expressed annoyance with your parents, however, though slight, strikes me as real, definitely coming from you. So let's change pace and talk about parents. Why is it difficult for your own to cut you loose?

Most of us parents are not sure that we did right by you, our children. So at least at a subconscious level we feel that if we're no more needed we're no more loved. These fears tell us to keep you needy, to treat you as if you were still two or three years younger than you are. You, on the other hand, particularly if you're safely in college, like to think of yourselves as some two or three years older than you are. That makes for a considerable age gap for successful communication.

What I suggest is to use your newfound

independence to demonstrate your continued affection. You said that you have a job at the post office over the Christmas vacation. You won't make a fortune, but you will make enough to take your Mom and Dad out for supper at a good restaurant. If you do, let me know what happened. It will be good, of that I'm sure.

After the vacation, we'll talk of Christmas, about how what's dangerous is not a commercialized but a sentimentalized Christmas.

Meanwhile, while on vacation give your mind the rest it richly deserves.

Merry Christmas,

Bill

get to see their fathers cry, for any reason, let alone for the continued love of a son?

I hope you're not as those who never cry. Listen. A short time ago I asked a friend, an eighty-five-year-old retired Yale professor, "What makes you cry?" He answered, "Whenever I see or hear the truth."

All wise people think tragically because tragedy teaches us less to indict and more to reflect. And reflections, particularly on personal sorrows that should include the sorrows of the world, stir deep emotions. At such moments tears are God-sent to cleanse the heart of bitterness, rage, and grief. In the eighty-fifth chapter of *Moby-Dick*, you'll find Melville's comment that "rainbows do not visit the clear air; they only irradiate vapor." Put differently, the heart would see no rainbow had the eye no tear.

I know you are far too deep to be a chirping optimist, but in being courageous stay clear of the stoicism that stunts your emotional growth.

As I recall, January is the time to bone up for the first semester finals. May you happily reach a peak of knowledge, and may each exam spark a new insight.

Bonne chance,

Bill

X

Dear Tom,

You haven't yet told me whether or not you ever cry, but you're right: I never did say why a sentimentalized Christmas is so much worse than a commercialized one.

The obvious answer is that the latter never pretends to be anything else. Sentimentality, however, does not arise from the truth; it's what's poured on top, blurring and distorting the truth.

Do you remember what I said about wise people thinking tragically? That's the way to think about Christmas. Let me draw a comparison.

The smallest street in Paris runs off the Seine river on the Left Bank near Notre Dame. It has a colorful name—*La rue du chat qui pêche* (The street of the cat who fishes). It is only a few yards long and very narrow.

Every summer thousands of tourists walk by, read the sign, and exclaim, "How picturesque." Were they, however, to go down the dank and sunless street, they would quickly conclude that the street of the cat who fishes is more suitable for cats than for human beings.

Now consider the Christmas crèche. The baby lies in the manger because no one in the inn would make room for a pregnant woman. The ox and the ass are not picturesque guests who just had to come and see; this is their home. The Christmas truth is that he who was to be the bread of life for human beings is laid in the feed box of animals.

At the beginning as at the end of Christ's life, God comes off wonderfully. We do not. The inhumanity, as we used to say, "of man to man" is exceeded only by man's inhumanity to God. That's why I think God is not too hard to believe in, just too good to believe in, we being strangers to such goodness.

After hearing confessions for half a century,

a priest concluded, "There aren't many grown-up people." Only the few who are have a mature understanding of Christmas and Good Friday. They are the ones who grasp the huge gifts and huge demands of Christianity.

By the time you receive this letter you'll have received your grades for the semester. You said you did your best; that's good enough. Don't let the grades tell you who you are!

As always I'm yours affectionately,

Bill

(2) because we learn less from success than from failure. It's really unfair, isn't it? As the kid complained: "Why are all the vitamins in the spinach and not in the ice cream?"

Do not fret about your prayer life. For the moment, a spiritual yearning suffices. Besides, everything is prayer. If you can see for yourself that "the world is charged with the grandeur of God"; if in certain times and places you can exclaim, "Heaven is under our feet as well as over our heads," you are praying, grateful for the awe and wonder of the natural world. If before entering your favorite class, or when sitting down each evening to do homework, you were to say, "For what I am about to receive, Lord, make me truly thankful," that would be a most appropriate prayer, for, as they used to say in the good-old-Latin-speaking days, *"Laborare est orare."* Work of all kinds done joyfully, thankfully, unselfishly, conscientiously—all such labor is prayer.

I can't stress wonder enough: "The world does not lack for wonder, only for a sense of wonder." So spoke Chesterton, and Huston Smith, another great religious scholar, used to insist, "The larger the island of knowledge the longer the shoreline of wonder."

Reading your letters assures me that you have not lost your sense of wonder. Without wonder prayer life is nil. So, as I say, don't fret.

Finally, when people complain that their prayers aren't answered, generally their prayers *are* answered and the answer is "No" and they haven't heard it. Life is, as they say in God's favorite tongue, *muy complicado.*

Abrazos,

Bill

PS: Another example of idol worship: Only Spanish-speaking folk think Spanish is God's favorite language. Americans are convinced it's English.

XII

Dear Tom,

I'm glad you have started going back to church "with a profound and critical humility." That will allow you to question all things earthly while being open to intuitions of some things heavenly!

At the wedding of my beloved stepson, his mother said a wonderful thing: "Put yourself in the way of beauty." By going to class you're putting yourself in the way of information and thought, and by going to church you're putting yourself in the way of gorgeous music and spiritual truths concerning yourself, the world, and God. Taking it all in is not of course automatic. Some people go to church to make their last stand against God. They don't worship God; they deify their own virtue. (Those damn idols again!)

My own advice for churchgoing is to experience first, soak in the hymns and anthems, the prayers and sermon—then only later, analyze.

Never become dogmatic. Dogma's fine—being dogmatic isn't; just as doctrines can be fine, being doctrinaire, never.

Allow your imagination free rein. Don't be

like some American jurists who carp constantly about what they call "original intent," about what exactly our forebears had in mind when writing the American Constitution. They remind me of a magic hour I once spent with an original copy of Beethoven's thirty-two piano sonatas. All the dynamics were there, even some fingering. Still, no two pianists play the sonatas alike. Interpretation is inevitable and, more than that, desirable. So it is with the Constitution and the Bible: we have both to recover tradition and to recover *from* it. Only so can the laws of our land and our religious beliefs remain meaningful.

Elie Wiesel once noted that "words can sometimes in moments of Grace, attain the qualities of 'deeds.'" I think he meant that words can truly empower us. This is true of biblical stories, of the Psalms, of the words of the prophets and the Gospels, not to mention St. Paul. And the stories don't all have to be literally true. "A myth," said Thomas Mann, "is a truth that is, and always will be, no matter how much we try to say it was." The truth of a myth is not literally true, only eternally so. The Bible is full of wonderfully imaginative myths like the one of Adam and Eve, and the story of their sons Cain and Abel. Cain kills Abel—the first recorded murder in the Bible is a fratricide! (Go interpret!)

The Bible dares my imagination to do more, more even than do Shakespeare and Blake. May it do the same for you in church and in the first-rate Bible course you say you intend to take.

I was moved by your telling me that while God is still a mystery, "Jesus is my kind of guy." Then let me end as did St. Paul in his first letter to the Corinthians: "The grace of the Lord Jesus Christ be with you."

Affectionately,

Bill

maid. When he asked, "How shall I declare my love?" his counselors answered, "Your majesty has only to appear in all the glory of your royal raiments before the maid's humble abode and she will instantly fall at your feet and be yours."

But it was precisely that thought that so troubled the king. He wanted her glorification, not his. In return for his love he wanted hers, freely given. The one thing he did not want was her submission to his power. What a dilemma: not to declare his love spelled the end of love, and to declare it spelled the end of his beloved! Finally, the king realized love's truth—that freedom for the beloved demanded equality with the beloved. So late one night, after all the counselors and courtiers of the palace had retired, he stole out a side door and appeared before the maid's cottage dressed as a servant.

Clearly the fable is a Christmas story and a lovely one. But let's not get carried away. I think the story, so satisfactory to its hero, and to its author Søren Kierkegaard, might well have been anything but satisfactory to its heroine. Had I been the maid, I would have wanted to know more about this stranger at my door, more about his future and mine. Was I to be stuck forever in the servants' quarters? Come to think of it, I don't mind a bit of submission. I don't mind marrying a king!

What do you think? I think most of us would much prefer God to remain God rather than become the frailest among us. We want God to be strong so that we can be weak. But God wants to be weak so that we can be strong.

The trouble with the usual notion of "Christian obedience" is that it represents a childhood model of living. Fearing confusion, a child naturally wants supervision and direction. A child wants a superior power to provide order and direct his destiny—and so do childish adults. But let's face that desire and call it what it is, namely, a temptation to disobedience. For we are called to obey not God's power, but God's love. God wants not submission to his power, but, in return for his love, our own.

It's all, as I said, wonderfully mysterious, but I suggest, Tom, that Jesus is "God's love in person on earth," and that God comes to earth as a child so that you and I and every other adult might finally grow up. You probably have seen Menotti's *Amahl and the Night Visitors.* Amahl, a crippled boy, is miraculously cured when he himself gives to the infant Jesus his crutch.

That's the Christmas present we should all bring to the manger: our crutches, our way of making God responsible for all the thinking and doing that we should be undertaking on our own. God provides minimum protection, but maximum support—support to help us grow up, to stretch our minds and hearts until they are as wide as God's universe. God doesn't want us narrow-minded, priggish, and subservient, but joyful

XIV

Dear Tom,

You question whether the Christian life is a happy one, for among your fellow students the "heathen" look happier than the Christians. I know what you're talking about, but in defense of Christian students let me say that religious faith often goes through three stages: conscious, self-conscious, and finally unconscious. That takes time. Only when you've reached the third stage are you free, and free perhaps to be really happy.

Actually I would call religious life joyful rather than happy. Happiness connotes pleasure while joy is a deeper emotion that, far from excluding, can actually include pain. Joy often points to a profound sense of self-fulfillment: "For this I was made and meant to be"—that's a joyful experience.

I remember being honored one Sunday afternoon—it was in 1967—by a telephone call from James Reston, the well-known *New York Times* columnist. He was writing his Monday morning column. He had been moved by my antiwar remarks on the steps of the Justice

Department where we were turning in draft cards, but he was feeling pessimistic. "I guess I'm too much a Calvinist, Reverend."

"No, Mr. Reston, you're no Calvinist; you're just gloomy. Calvinists are animated by hope."

"What's that?"

"Hope reflects the state of your soul rather than the circumstances surrounding your days. Praise God and your soul gets stronger."

We had a good theological conversation about Christian hope, but Monday's column was still pretty gloomy.

Joy doesn't exclude happiness. In the Gospel of John, Jesus first visits people not in their suffering but at a wedding feast at Cana. Whether or not you believe he changed the water into wine, it's clear that he came down solidly on the side of happiness.

According to Karl Barth, the great Swiss theologian, the gospel, which as you know means *good* not bad news, is not "impenetrable darkness" but "indescribable light." It's the kind of light of which St. John wrote, "The light shines in the darkness, and the darkness has not overcome it."

Far from gloomy, Christians are called "children of light." They believe that "the light for all time shall outspeed the thundercrack" (William Carlos Williams). They find joy and support in the ordinary things of life, as does my poet neighbor Jim Schley:

Though dark is pressing down

    see what lasts—

The evenhanded decency of daylight.

Actually, if only one-tenth of what Christians believe were true, we Christians should be ten times as excited as we are! To be sure we're often sad, heartbroken years ago by the war in Vietnam and now by the madness of American foreign policy. But we're never gloomy. Those who are more intent on quenching the bonfires of sin than on fanning the embers of creativity—these are poor examples of Christianity. "The glory of God is a human being fully alive," wrote Irenaeus, an early Christian.

And gratitude, not obedience, is the primary religious emotion. Duty calls only when gratitude fails to prompt.

Before closing I want to say that I cheered out loud when you said that you and your father had had a wonderful exchange of letters after the Christmas vacation. That represents both happiness and joy.

As each day unfolds, dear Tom, may you see less of the shadow and more of the sun.

Your old (quite) friend,

Bill

But hey! Have mercy. Substance takes time; provocation, far less. Letters are not books. If my letters provoke you to tackle some seasoned writings for the good of your soul, my mission is accomplished. And please never forget that if my letters to you are occasionally not profitable, your letters to me are always pleasurable, containing fine, heartwarming insights.

You still puzzle about happiness being in tension with "sins of the flesh." Bearing in mind your admonishment not to be merely provocative, I'll try to give you an abundance of wisdom in an economy of words! St. Paul is the only biblical writer who uses the phrase, and the New Testament has two words for "flesh": one is *sōma,* the Greek word for "body," e.g., "psychosomatic"; the other is *sarx*. When Paul talks of the sins of the flesh, he uses the word *sarx*. In the fifth chapter of his letter to the Galatians he lists them: "fornication, impurity, licentiousness, idolatry, sorcery, enmities, strife, jealousy, anger, quarrels, dissensions, factions, envy, drunkenness, carousing, and things like these." Now you tell me: Do these sins of the flesh arise out of your lower body or higher up, from your spirit, from the realm of freedom and the misuse of it? Granted that unconscious drives affect our freedom, as do our human frailties, still freedom is where decisions are made. Therefore sins essentially represent freedom abused.

Actually, it's better to think of sins in the singular. Sin is separation, a state of being in which we are alienated from God, from one another, and from our real and loving selves. Sin is rending the bond of love, and its punishment is experiencing the bond of love rent. Read *Crime and Punishment,* for Dostoyevsky writes poignantly of all this, in fact so movingly that *Crime and Punishment* almost singlehandedly converted me to Christianity. What you need to know is that Raskolnikov, the novel's main character, is a name carefully chosen. In Russian a *raskolnik* can mean either a split personality or a heretic. The novel could have been as easily entitled *Orthodoxy and Heresy.*

As your weekdays seem full of things that matter, give yourself a little slack on weekends.

You don't want to become gloomy, and happiness is a much-neglected virtue.

As per usual, much love,

Bill

Francis Macomber, "He had a great tolerance about him, which would have been a virtue had it not been so insidious."

I myself came away from the movie weeping. What so struck me was the way once again the rich and powerful do as they will, while the poor and powerless suffer as they must. Nowadays rich Republicans say to the poor, "What's in our self-interest is in your interest." Obviously that's not true of all of them, but the generosity of the many hardly makes up for the greed of the rest. Rich Republicans claim government services breed dependency, but is inheriting millions good for the grit in their souls? My own feeling is that just as the poor should not be left at the mercy of their poverty, so the rich should not be left at the mercy of their wealth.

So large these days are the problems of our society and of the world, that our own personal failings often seem paltry by comparison. I remember once asking a priest, whose parish included a nearby convent, what it was like listening to the confessions of nuns. He answered, "It's like being stoned to death with popcorn"—a reminder that national trespasses can far exceed our interpersonal ones.

You ask what I think of President Bush's Christianity. I think his God is too violent, hardly the God to whom Christ prayed. And I think his God is too small. It's a fundamental Christian conviction that all of us in this world belong one to another. That's the way God made us; Christ died to keep us that way; our sin is only and always that we put asunder what God has joined together.

For every serious believer, that raises the question "Who is there big enough to love the whole world?" How can the President call Iran, Iraq, and North Korea "the axis of evil" when the whole of humanity suffers infinitely more from environmental degradation, pandemic poverty, and a world awash with weapons?

I don't doubt that, in sobering up, the President had a religious conversion. But I doubt that he realizes that a personal religious conversion demands a change in social attitudes. Jesus put first those whom society counted least and put last. He was "the servant of the poor." Yet President Bush's "compassionate conservatism" seems primarily reserved for CEOs and unborn babies. Once born, and if poor, these children need doctors and schools far more than generals and war. It's now the case that the number of homeless children in the United States is higher than at any time since records began to be kept in the late 1970s.

And how can a Christian president remain so indifferent to the harm brought to poor African and South American farmers by American tariffs and subsidies that protect our own big landowners?

I'm not saying that capitalism is anti-Christian; that's too simple. What I am saying is that social justice is central to the gospel, not ancillary to it. Economic justice is one of the main pillars upholding the whole edifice of society, as Adam Smith himself insisted. His "invisible hand" took for granted a just society. He also believed capitalism works better when individual merit trumps inherited wealth.

It's hard to square Christianity with the heartless neglect of people in need. Too much of what passes for Christianity substitutes emotions for morals. Too much is lip service. And giving lip service to God doesn't advance faith; it weakens it.

A final word, or rather a question. I read that in 2003 Vice President Cheney sent a Christmas card to the President, a commentary on verse 29 of Matthew 10. The card read, "And if a sparrow cannot fall to the ground without His notice, is it probable that an empire can rise without His aid?"

What say you?

Bill

PS: You made my heart glad by appreciating the role of anger in the works of love.

XVII

Dear Tom,

I'm glad the VP's Christmas card stirred up such deep and informed feelings about empire building and wars. Actually you are way ahead of where I was at eighteen. My eagerness to fight Hitler was totally uncritical. Never did it occur to me that fighting fire with fire might produce only more ashes. I considered World War II a necessary evil, and I think I still do. However, I now realize, particularly in the nuclear age, that war, like most necessary evils, is far more evil than necessary.

I loved your remembering from high school days what a jaundiced Caesar says in Shaw's *Caesar and Cleopatra*: "And so to the end of history, murder shall breed murder, always in the name of right and honor and peace, until at last the gods tire of blood and create a race that can understand."

Are you really going to send that quote to Cheney? Be sure you do, and add one of Thomas Mann's: "War is a coward's escape from the problems of peace."

Just don't bet the bank on a reply. I'm a big believer in the beatitude that reads, "Blessed are they who do not expect too much, for they shall not so soon be disappointed."

I don't want to leave Jesus' sparrow without a word of explanation. I think I cited St. Matthew in my last letter. In St. Luke's Gospel, Jesus asks, "Are not five sparrows sold for two pennies? Yet not one of them is forgotten in God's sight."

In those days the rich bought animals to sacrifice while the poor could afford only sparrows. Sparrows went two for a penny, and if you bought two pennies' worth, a fifth was thrown in.

God cares for that fifth sparrow, the one tossed in! Nature is made the symbol of God's supernatural mercy. It is with an unbounded, unfathomable love that God loves every last human being on the face of the earth from the

Pope to the loneliest wino. "Do not be afraid," adds Jesus, "you are of more value than many sparrows." And God's love doesn't seek value; it creates it. It's not because we have value that we are loved, but because we are loved that we have value. Our value is a gift, not an achievement. Just think: we never have to prove ourselves; that's already taken care of. All we have to do is to express ourselves—return God's love with our own—and what a world of difference there is between proving ourselves and expressing ourselves.

You remember months ago I asked you— prematurely to be sure—what it would be like to have God tell you who you are? I've just given you my own answer. I never get over the huge gift and huge demands of Christianity, the gift of

God's love and the demands of human possibility. Christianity has certainly not been tried and found wanting; it has been tried and found difficult, and watered down again and again.

The founding pastor of Riverside Church in New York once wrote, "The world has tried in two ways to get rid of Jesus: first, by crucifying him, and second, by worshiping him." Jesus doesn't ask us to worship him. He said, "Follow me." Faith is a matter of being faithful. It's not believing without proof; it's trusting without reservation. No easy task. But faithfulness is joyful. As you have sung more than once in Handel's *Messiah*, "My yoke is easy and my burden is light." (There's no paradox like a biblical one!)

I sure wish we could make music again as

XVIII

Dear Tom,

If I'm correct, in two days you'll turn nine-teen. Happy Birthday! Or should I wish you as do the Poles their Polish pope: *"Sta let"*—May you live to be a hundred?

I think I'll withdraw the latter wish as the goal of reaching one hundred must sound as dis-tant to you as it does exhausting to me.

Instead let's go back again to that memorable visit two summers ago. When we were playing those three Schubert sonatas, you stumbled over a few notes but never fell. It was as if you knew that notes were important but that phrasing was everything.

Your playing then strikes me as a metaphor for your life now. Today you are mastering fact after fact, but it's the scheme, the design of things that seems to interest you most. No amount of trees obscures your view of the forest. That's wonderful.

The other thing that stands out in my memory is your humor, which now glows brightly in your letters. Beyond the fun of it, people don't always realize how indispensable humor is to a better future. Laughing, as you do, at the stock notions and habits of the rich and powerful is a way of changing perceptions, a first step in realigning power. As Faulkner used to say in the old days of Southern segregation, "Make us look silly."

Of course, in your case, I could worry about sophomore year just around the bend. It's often viewed as prime time for cynicism, self-absorption, and carelessness. But I'm sure your humor plus your compassion will see you through.

So once again, "Happy Birthday." Enjoy it. Celebrate it. As the fox said to the little prince, "We must have rites." Here in the deep snows of Vermont I'll raise a glass of Russia's finest and hope that your new year may be the best yet.

Cheers,

Bill

XIX

Dear Tom,

Your roommate just called to tell me that
your closest buddy throughout all your high
school years died today in a car crash. I'm very,
very sorry. Cry profusely; be angry; you won't
fall apart.

I do hope you and your friends speak at
Seth's memorial service. It will mean a lot to his

parents to know how much their son meant to you. I'll write when you get back.

Bill

XX

Dear Tom,

I didn't call because we're communicating by letter—after the dust settles. I was hoping to hear from you but figured it was too early for the long letter you would feel constrained to write. I so wanted to learn about the service, and how the parents and you and your friends were coping with your loss.

For Seth's parents in particular it's important to realize that what they've lost is not only a son; they have also lost a host of expectations. It's tough but crucial to confront this part of their loss. For Seth himself, they have freely to grieve, and I would suggest talking to him all the time. That's what did a lot for me when my own son Alex was killed in a car accident. He was twenty-four and at the wheel. At his funeral, his younger brother David addressed him magnificently, "You blew it, buddy, you blew it, and just when I was getting to love you." All his fellow athletes, fellow bartenders, waiters and waitresses nodded in approval.

Months later David talked to him again with similar eloquence. It was a hot summer day, and

But then, from the back of the chapel, the priest taking the service began to intone the famous words from Job: "The Lord gave, and the Lord hath taken away; blessed be the name of the Lord."

He sounded nauseatingly pious. Looking around, I could see him coming down the aisle, his nose in the prayer book. I resolved to trip him up. However, as I was getting ready to stick my leg out, a small voice, as it were, asked me, "What part of the phrase, Coffin, are you objecting to?" I thought it was the second part: "The Lord hath taken away." Then suddenly it dawned on me that I was protesting the first: "The Lord gave." It hit me hard that it was not my world; that at best we were all guests. And "The Lord gave" was a statement against which all the spears of human pride have to be hurled and shattered.

Literally, of course, the Lord had not taken anybody away. No one knows enough to say that. Why should I survive and not you? God doesn't go around the world with his hands on steering wheels, his fist around knives, his finger on triggers. On 9/11 He watched in horror, His heart the first of all our hearts to break. Come to think of it, the whole surface of the earth is soaked with the tears and blood of the innocent, almost all of it our doing. The one thing we can hold up against God is giving us our freedom. You remember what the priest said: "There are few grown-ups." So, if you give a small child an expensive watch and he smashes it, whose the fault?

Still, if love is the name of the game, freedom is the precondition. Freedom may be a burden; choice scary, but it belongs to us. It's ours to use or abuse.

If you're up for advice, do what psychiatrists call "grief-work"; play your fiddle, read some psalms and other poems. The one that released the floodgates for me was A. E. Housman's "To an Athlete Dying Young." Again, you won't fall apart.

Write a line or two just to tell me how you are. And remember, Seth too would not wish to be held close by grief alone. Better to remember him by furthering his highest hopes.

A big hug,

Bill

XXI

Dear Tom,

I'm grateful that you made the effort to write, and such a good letter too. That the service for Seth was moving was predictable. What surprised and pleased me deeply was your playing the adagio from Bach's G Minor unaccompanied sonata. What solace, what sanity in Bach.

Seth's mother and father, I'm sure, were

touched by the tributes of his classmates and teachers. Of course they made them cry. In the long run, however, there's comfort in realizing how much in his tragically short life their son meant to so many. Now for them come hard times.

There's a story told of a Chinese emperor who asked his wise man to define happiness. When the man couldn't, the emperor gave him a month to think it over. When he returned, and after the emperor had asked him once again, "What is happiness?" the wise man answered, "Happiness is when the grandfather dies, then the father, and then the son."

It's when the sequence gets fouled up that the pain becomes so acute. But then when unbearable grief turns into bearable sorrow, an important decision has to be made. Either you stay stuck in your own sorrow, or your heart can widen to embrace the comparable sorrow of others. It's a crucial choice, for without doubt the best healers in this world are wounded healers.

America as a whole has gone through a comparable experience following 9/11. We were deeply wounded and felt unfairly so. That feeling could have led to a deep kinship for other people who had suffered as had we, and more. But instead we succumbed to feelings of being victimized. The number one superpower of the world became the number one victim of the world. I think we still resent our lost sense of invincibility and invulnerability. As both were and you feel you should have helped him do so. You also feel that by driving too fast he was flirting with suicide, feelings you might have helped allay.

All this may be true, in which case you have my understanding and deep sympathies. After World War II in Germany I had the chance to save the lives of many Russian POWs being forcefully repatriated to the Soviet Union. I could have done so but in cowardly fashion obeyed orders instead. It's a burden I've carried for sixty years.

What's important, Tom, are three things. First, think again of our conversations about forgiveness. Second, if you have the experience and don't miss the meaning, the memory of your failure with Seth will help you help many others in ways now unpredictable. Finally, every death of a loved one reminds us of something we should have said or done but didn't. So all of us standing in need of God's mercy are forced to conclude, "It's finished; even the unfinished is finished."

One more thought. If you still have doubts about gays and lesbians, try out this possibility: it's always a good time to change your mind when to do so will widen your heart.

Tender mercies,

Bill

XXII

Dear Tom,

The letter I mailed yesterday should have included the following open letter to America's Catholic Bishops, written four years ago. If I had been smarter and better able to do so, I would have addressed "natural law" rather than the Bible.

Cheers,

Bill

Enclosure

AN OPEN LETTER TO THE ROMAN CATHOLIC BISHOPS OF AMERICA

NOVEMBER 14, 2000

In a Washington cemetery, on the gravestone of a Vietnam veteran, it is written, "When I was in the military, they gave me a medal for killing two men and a discharge for loving one."

Why, like the army, are so many churches on the wrong side of history? Why is a man loving another immutably immoral? Can a Hamlet once again persuade a reluctant Horatio that "there are more things in heaven and earth, Horatio, than are dreamt of in your philosophy"?

As we have done in other cities, addressing the leaders of other Christian denominations, so, from St. Paul and to retain passages from a mis-read Old Testament law code. Everything biblical is not Christlike, and these particular verses, involving more hate than love, have no place whatsoever in the human heart. For Christians, the problem is not how to reconcile homosexuality with scriptural passages that condemn it, but how to reconcile the rejection and punishment of homosexuals with the love of Christ. If people can show the tenderness and constancy in caring that honors Christ's love, what matters their sexual orientation? Shouldn't a relationship be judged by its inner worth rather than by its outer appearance? Shouldn't a Christian sexual ethic focus on personal relationships and social justice rather than particular sexual acts, particularly when evidence increasingly emerges that homosexuality is a natural biological variation?

I'm a great believer in tradition. It's a big mistake casually to discount Church doctrines that once convinced the wisest among our Christian forebears. But doctrines are not immune to error; tradition is no oracle. And a tradition that cannot be changed also cannot be preserved. That lesson is as old as history itself. In other words, church people have always both to recover tradition and to recover *from* it.

I know that the Roman Catholic Church repudiates violent forms of homophobia. But to deplore the violence while continuing to proclaim the ideas that undergird it strikes thoughtful people as hypocritical. The teaching of the Church encourages the denigration of gays and lesbians. So instead of looking at gays and lesbians from the perspective of Catholic theology, wouldn't it be better to look at Catholic theology from the perspective of gays and lesbians? The picture of Matthew Shepard hanging on a Wyoming fence burns in my mind and heart.

Said Edmund Burke, "Falsehood has a perennial spring." And why not? "Our knowledge is imperfect"; "We see in a mirror, dimly." Isn't that why the revelation of Jesus is finally about loving rather than knowing?

I close with another image, one that has haunted me for fifty years. Albert Camus complained of Christians who climb up on the cross to be seen from afar, thereby trampling on the One who has hung there so long.

Were you moved to respond I would be deeply grateful.

William Sloane Coffin

Spirituality takes many forms, but a politically engaged spirituality is today crucial.

The separation of church and state does not mean the divorce of a Christian from his politics. And if anyone claims he or she is above politics, they're in effect for the status quo—a very political position.

You note some vexing issues, cultural as well as political, and astutely ask: If changing my mind would widen my heart, then isn't it time for me to rethink my position on abortion?

Interesting point. But there are some problems. First of all, questions about abortion really should be addressed to women. Men can't pretend to be as intimately involved. What men *can* do, along with women, is to try to raise the presently abysmal level of discourse on the whole subject.

To be remembered is that while the law may have to reach a decision, a decision is not a definition, and science is no more helpful. Science can tell us when a heart starts beating and when a brain is dead. But when human life begins and when it ends—these are not medical judgments but rather moral mysteries and as such can be scientifically neither proven nor disproven.

Also, for every Roman Catholic, fundamentalist Protestant, and Orthodox Jew who holds that an unborn child is from the very first a child, there are other Roman Catholics who believe that life in the womb has to be "ensouled" before it becomes human (the more traditional Catholic developmental view of St. Thomas Aquinas), as there are countless more believers and nonbelievers alike who believe that human life begins with the first breath. That raises a serious question: How in a democracy can you make a crime what the majority of citizens don't even consider a sin?

Moreover, to criminalize abortion would not of itself instill a sense of the sanctity of prenatal life. And if criminalizing abortion would reduce the legal abortions but not significantly the total number of abortions, the result would be more emotionally than morally satisfying.

One of the criteria for a good law is its enforceability. An antiabortion law would probably prove as unenforceable as the Prohibition laws of the 1920s, which we finally repealed in 1933.

Further, a widened heart, as I suggested, would take very much into account the individual feelings and concerns of women. This should be particularly remembered by men. To say of a mother in the slums of Rio or Chicago, with more children than resources to keep them alive and well, that her decision to have an abortion has the "moral malice of murder" is sheer nonsense. Every doctrine is in danger of divorcing motive from action, of becoming abstract and therefore cruel. And many, many women who are convinced that they have the right to an abortion will also tell you that the sorrow of losing a potential child for whatever reason haunts them for the rest of their lives. Abortion is a dreadful experience, and whether or not to have one is not for the state

But evil has an irremedial stubborness about it. It has to be recognized, and that always includes recognizing our own complicity in it. (Said Augustine, "Never fight evil as if it were something that arose totally outside of yourself.") It also has to be constrained, but never, I think, can it be eliminated. The pacifists I most admire are those who recognize that the mystery of evil is beyond their solution. That means, given the disastrous unintended consequences of just about every war, we all have dilemmas.

Wars are harder and harder these days to call "just." But what about a just revolution? A just humanitarian intervention authorized by the UN? Personally I look forward to a future when national armies will be disbanded, their places taken by an international police force whose size, shape, command, and authority are impossible now to predict.

I said my vote was 51-49, but increasingly I'm with Psalm 33: "The war horse is a vain hope for victory, and by its great might it cannot save."

Actually the Bible is ambiguous about the use of force. What *is* wrong—always wrong—is the desire to use it.

I am beginning to think that you need, less and less, pointers from me.

God bless you.

Bill

XXIV

Dear Tom,

I was hoping you wouldn't ask for my views on terrorism. They overflow the limits of a letter. I'll try to be succinct.

Terrorism is a clear and present danger, but our present policies are nourishing rather than restraining terrorists. This is particularly true of the war against Iraq. And let's not forget what an

Israeli journalist wrote: "The terrorism of suicide bombers is born of despair. There is no military solution to despair."

Armed forces are generally an ineffective and often counterproductive weapon against terror. Norman Mailer compared our present pursuit of terrorists to a Sherman tank going after a hornet hiding in a building. By the time the building is flattened, arousing considerable resentment, the hornet is safely in the attic next door.

The Defense Department claims there are al-Qaeda cells today in some sixty nations. That's why we can't be indifferent to the skyrocketing anti-Americanism our unilateral actions have provoked. Better by far to be bound, as the

Declaration of Independence put it, by "a decent respect for the opinions of mankind." With cells in sixty nations we need allies, lots of them, who think not ill but well of us. We need sturdy partners with whom to share intelligence, to freeze assets, and, if internationally sanctioned, to engage together in preemptive action not against individual states but against individual terrorists, to bring them to trial before an international court like the International Criminal Court we have wrongfully refused to join.

Most of all, we must agree to be governed by the force of law, not by the law of force.

Also, while seeking to contain the effects of terrorism, we need to understand what produces it. Terrorism is no metaphysical abstraction; it springs from historical causes—political oppression, economic deprivation, spiritual humiliation, and, as the Israeli journalist said, despair.

That suggests that in dealing with terrorism the issue of justice rather than security should be primary. In today's world, even more than in previous years, ostentatious wealth lives cheek by jowl with devastating poverty, and globalization is institutionalizing the inequity. Wouldn't America's national security actually be enhanced if we spent some of the Pentagon's billions fighting the poverty of the third and fourth worlds? Wouldn't that lower the hatred of America, slow down the recruitment of terrorists? Wouldn't such a policy start to refill the reservoir of America's moral authority seen by billions today as bone-dry?

What makes such a proposed change of course so difficult is that it demands a profound change of heart. Not only must the mind-set of our leaders be changed but also the mentality of so many Americans. Addressing the Air Force Academy, the President said, "No act of America explains terrorist violence." That is an incredibly naive analysis, but most Americans are buying it. They believed the President when in 2002 in Crawford, Texas, he said, "Our nation is the greatest force for good in history." This amounts to believing in American ideals untouched by American practices. It is an absurd conceit. Republicans and Democrats alike—we have to get over this kind of thinking; we have to escape this web of self-deception and self-celebration.

your heart these words of British philosopher John Ruskin: "The primary reward for human toil is not what you get for it, but what you become by it." As a suburban lifeguard you may become a car owner and even a bit more charming (as if your charm were in short supply). But what else?

Let me tell you a story. Years ago when I was university chaplain there taught on campus a well-known scholar of American literature. He was from Louisiana, white, and a bit of a racist.

In 1961 I was a member of a small racially mixed group of so-called "freedom riders," trying to desegregate interstate bus travel. We were arrested and jailed in Montgomery, Alabama. As it was a pretty tumultuous time, the incident received widespread publicity, and as a consequence I received a lot of hate mail ("commie," "nigger-lover," "outside agitator," etc.). There were also some friendly letters and one in particular I loved. It came from an elderly white woman who lived in New Orleans. She had marched, pretty much on her own, through the swamps of segregation only to emerge on the other side with far more knowledge and obvious credibility than was generally ascribed to us "Northern liberals." (You have to remember that for decades, to be a prointegration white in the South was comparable to being an anticommunist Russian in the Soviet Union.)

This woman and I became pen pals, and in the course of our correspondence she revealed that she was the mother-in-law of the well-known university scholar I mentioned.

Eventually she came north to visit her daughter. I invited her to lunch, and she regaled me with tragic/inspiring tales of black/white relations in New Orleans. At the end of lunch I suggested that her distinguished son-in-law might not go along with all her views. At that, with the sweetest possible smile, she took her distinguished son-in-law out at the knees. She said, "No, he wouldn't go along with all my views. But you see, he was born conservative and has never had an important experience."

Born conservative and has never had an important experience: wouldn't you call that a pretty fair description of a lot of university students today? I'm convinced every first-world student should have a third-world experience, either abroad or here in the states. Abroad, American students would find out firsthand what poverty and economic exploitation are all about, and why all third-world citizens should really be given a vote for the American president, so great on their countries is the impact of American foreign policy.

A third-world experience at home would sharpen insights and deepen convictions about what the country needs. Almost all today's students agree that "all men [people] are created equal." But how many *feel* the monstrosity of inequality? That's another type of knowledge altogether.

These are the kinds of important experiences some very bright students and faculty lack. Moreover, what has become of your growing interest in politics? It's an election year, man, arguably the most crucial presidential election since 1932. If, instead of sitting by a suburban pool you went door-to-door in a poor city district, you would certainly hear points of view far different from what you're used to, and you would be useful to boot.

You are a topflight student, Tom, in a torch-carrying university. But you have to experience far more of life. Values are less taught than caught, caught in "important experiences." Ethical principles and moral theories motivate no one. Empathy and courage spring from the heart.

Remember that the greatest perils to the planet arise not from the poor and ignorant for whom education is an answer; they are caused by the well-educated for whom self-interest is the problem. And I'll tell you something else: action tends to lead to more new ways of thinking than does thought to new ways of acting.

Why do I sound overwrought? Because at every spring commencement I used to ask myself, "After their years here, are our students more or less concerned about their neighbors' needs?"

I concluded that the humanities for too many students were but cultural icing on an economic cake, especially when "enrich thyself" is the country's prevailing ethos.

unwanted, and by people, friendly and not so friendly. I myself have often been forced down by people for whom compassion was the last thing on their mind. Call such experiences "severe mercies." They have taught me that I am more alive in pain than in complacency. (We're back to the "joy" of self-fulfillment.)

Maybe I am deluded by my longing to have you among the people the priest considered "grown-ups." That's why I wanted you to put yourself in the way of the big things of which real living consists. Today poverty worldwide is a big thing. So is keeping the world from destroying itself and stopping humanity from ravaging the earth as if there were no tomorrow. Let's not kid ourselves: the planet is not going to endure our insults forever. So once again "who is there big enough to love the whole world?"

We're talking again about a politically engaged spirituality. In churches, Christ is always in danger of being domesticated. Too many members think of him as a sort of first-century Fred Rogers. Not always, but often I think of him as the Christ of whom someone in anguish asked, "Whither, relentless, wilt thou still be driving thy maimed and halt that have not strength to go?"

Reading and rereading your letters, I am full of admiration at the way, in the spirit of Rilke, you have loved the questions. Now, you must *live* the questions and begin, as Rilke suggested, to live into the answers. These are many, but they are essentially ethical as is the reality of human existence.

The most important truths in life are to be found in human relations, not in facts and figures. The leap of faith is not a leap of thought but of action. As I wrote earlier, faith is not believing without proof; it's trusting without reservation, life being impossible to live fully without trust. You have to act wholeheartedly without absolute certainty. And everything worthwhile is difficult—yes, even grace, which is more than a blessing; it's a challenge. You have to become responsible—response-able.

Don't groan; it's fulfilling to live life to the full. It's boring not to. You don't want to become a spiritual midget. If you do become a Christian, be a big one. That's what I long for you. To repeat old Irenaeus, "The glory of God is a human being fully alive."

You ask about my health. I have known better days but none happier. My spirits are high and everything else is commentary.

Thanks for asking, and forgive me for hurting your feelings.

Love,

Bill

Dear Tom,

Don't worry. Already the more-than-usual interval between letters said you needed a respite. And apparently you would appreciate the respite continuing as you want to turn my attention to what you call "that special art form," the sermon. Preaching has also been called "truth through personality." Bear in mind once again that a letter is not a book, and I'll comply, listing a few things I used to think about when writing, delivering, and listening to sermons.

1. No souls are saved after twenty minutes. That statement would be rejected out of hand by every black Baptist preacher in the country and certainly by Jonathan Edwards, who nearly three hundred years ago in nearby Northampton used to hold forth for almost two hours every Sunday.

If the sermon is interesting, I listen to it with pleasure and profit no matter what its length. But for me, twenty minutes was the limit, with about an hour of preparation for every minute of preaching.

2. A good sermon is like a good whodunit; the surprise is the discovery of inevitability. I

actually once saw a person in the second pew slap his thigh as if to say, "Of course, why didn't I think of that?" Successful preaching raises to a conscious level the knowledge inherent in people's lives. That's why you preach for, not at, people.

3. The best sermons are based on biblical texts; seldom are they topical. And preachers should not go to work on the texts; they should allow the texts to go to work on them. Listening is the first exercise in understanding.

4. Dignity is never obtained at the expense of specificity. Preachers typically generalize when trying to avoid controversial issues. They do so primarily for two reasons:

    a. They haven't done their homework

and so don't know what to say. If their ignorance stems from their complacency, it is an ethical, not an intellectual, default.

b. They don't want to jeopardize their congregation's affection for them. A true friend of course is one willing to risk his friendship for the sake of his friend, rather than to use his friend for the sake of the friendship. Imagine considering yourself a good pastor yet being so timid as to say not a word about homosexuality, the most divisive issue to rend the churches since slavery.

5. Controversial issues should be broached with great pastoral care. For instance, there is nothing to stop a preacher in the middle of a sermon from saying, "What I now want to say is not easy for me to say, so I can imagine how painful

it will be for some of you to hear. But here we are in church where unity is based not on agreement but on mutual concern. So let me tell you what's on my mind and heart, and after the service you tell me where you think I went wrong."

6. It is well to remember what St. Augustine wrote: "There are as many wolves within the fold as there are sheep without." If you are a true shepherd of the flock, what are you going to do with all those wolves? I leave to you to answer the question "Like what?" My concern here is for preachers to be constantly aware of the sheep, browsing on hillsides, wondering when they can safely return to the sheepfold.

7. Never scold. Pour contempt but never scold. That's what the biblical prophets did. So

did Jesus, who, though he was more than a prophet, was never anything less.

8. Preaching is about God's love and human possibility. Faith puts people on the road, hope keeps them there, and love indeed makes the world go around. Despair is not an option.

9. "Rejoice with those who rejoice, weep with those who weep." Be rich in emotion, strong in conviction, and tender as only the truly strong can be tender. Love your congregation, and

10. Be the first to do what your sermon calls for. If you can't persuade yourself, how will you persuade others?

Maybe at the end of Holy Week I'll send you an Easter sermon. If it arrives late, no matter; Easter is a season, not a day.

May the Lord's face shine upon you. Mine does with love.

Bill

PS: Speaking of good whodunits, Vermont boasts a fine writer of such books, Archer Mayor. At the end of *Tucker Peak* he offers a view of life I would commend to all preachers. Musing on human malfeasance in a corrupt world, detective Joe Gunther sighs, "God, what a species we are."

Sheriff Dawson smiles: "You gotta love it."

famous line of Faust's: "Moment, ah still delay, thou art so fair."

By the time you read this letter, however, the moment may have begun to fade. Maybe it's all for the best, for

> "Go, go, go," said the bird,
> "Humankind cannot bear much reality."

After all you've been through, I hesitate to send you another Easter sermon. But, as promised, here it is; I preached it some twenty years ago at Riverside Church in New York City.

Before closing I want to tell you that I was touched by your change in summer plans, particularly because you didn't have to tell me. I agree completely that we all have weak moments when we are, as you put it, "immensely suggestible." As the Buddhists say, you can't stop certain thoughts from coming to mind, but you don't have to invite them to tea.

May your teatime, or happy hour, or late-night beer, whatever, be filled with happy thoughts.

Cheers,

Bill

LIKE HIM WE RISE

READINGS: MATTHEW 28
1 CORINTHIANS 15:17–18, 20

In Haydn's oratorio *The Seasons,* in the section called "Spring," the chorus sings, "As yet the year is unconfirmed, and oft-returning winter's blast the bud and bloom destroy"—an apt description of this blustery day. But no matter: we know that energy soon will be pouring out of the ground and into every blade of grass; into every flower, bush, and tree; we know that soon the robins will join the pigeons, the sky will be full of the thunder of the sun, "the shaggy mountains will stomp their feet, the waves toss high and clap their wild blue hands." Overhead and underfoot and all around we shall soon see, hear, feel, and smell the juice and joy of spring.

But suppose this horrible weather were here to stay. Suppose that April had never come, that the earth somehow had spun out of orbit and was headed for the immensities of space, there forever to be assailed by winter's blasts. Not only would that be a gruesome prospect, but also, according to St. Paul, a proper analogy for the state of human affairs without Easter. Not one to hedge his bets, St. Paul puts all his Christian eggs in one Easter basket: "If Christ has not been raised, your faith is futile" (1 Cor. 15:17). Just as we know that April is coming, despite all appearances, because April is already here, so we know that we no longer live in a

Good Friday world because Easter is already here.

God knows it continues to look like a Good Friday world. What makes the Good Friday story so devastating is that it is still so shockingly true. In totalitarian countries politicians have but to hear, "Thou art not Caesar's friend" (John 19:12 KJV), and away they fall like autumn leaves. In more democratic countries, politicians seek to minimize their responsibilities, washing their hands and thereby plaiting the crown of thorns. Like Peter, most of us disciples follow our Lord halfway, but not the other half. As for the majority of citizens, are they not like the crowd that gathered on Calvary, not to cheer a miscarriage of justice, but also not to protest it? Failing to realize that compassion without confrontation is hopelessly sentimental, the people go home beating their breasts, preferring guilt to responsibility.

By all appearances, it is a Good Friday world. But by the light of Easter, through the thick darkness covering the nations, we can dimly discern a "Yes, but" kind of message. Yes, fear and self-righteousness, indifference and sentimentality kill; but love never dies, not with God, and not even with us. The Easter message says that all the tenderness and strength that on Good Friday we saw scourged, buffeted, stretched out on a cross—all that beauty and goodness is again alive and with us now, not as a memory that inevitably fades, but as an undying presence in the life of every single one of us, if airy and sweet. But there's nothing sentimental about Easter: Easter represents a demand as well as a promise, a demand not that we sympathize with the crucified Christ, but that we pledge our loyalty to the risen One. That means an end to all loyalties, to all people, and to all institutions that crucify. I don't see how you can proclaim allegiance to the risen Lord and then allow life once again to lull you to sleep, to smother you in convention, to choke you with success. It seems to me that the burden of proof is with those who think they can combine loyalty to the risen Christ with continuing the arms race; or with those who think that we Americans have the right to decide who lives, dies, and rules in other countries; or with those who think that the risen Lord would not argue with an economic system that clearly reverses the priorities of Mary's Magnificat—filling the rich with good things and sending the poor away empty.

True loyalty to the risen Lord is surely that displayed by Peter, who finally went the second half, who became ten times the person he was before Jesus' death. It is the loyalty of St. Stephen, who wasn't afraid of confrontation, and who under the rain of death-dealing stones cried out, Christlike, "Father, forgive"; the loyalty of so many early Christian men and women who, like Peter and Stephen, watered with their blood the seed of the church until it became the acorn that broke the mighty boulder that was the Roman Empire.

There is an Easter sunrise service that takes place on the edge of the Grand Canyon. As the scripture line is read, "And suddenly there was a great earthquake; for an angel of the Lord, descending from heaven, came and rolled back the stone" (Matt. 28:2), a giant boulder is heaved over the rim. As it goes crashing down the side of the Grand Canyon into the Colorado River far below, a two-thousand-voice choir bursts into the Hallelujah chorus. Too dramatic? Not if, despite all appearances, we live in an Easter world.

But let's move on with St. Paul's under-standing of Easter: "If Christ has not been raised, your faith is futile and you are still in your sins" (1 Cor. 15:17). I don't know why sin is such a bad word these days. Obviously, we're all sinners, the more so the more we try to deny it. But that's not the issue. At issue is whether there is more mercy in God than sin in us. And according to Paul, just as love is stronger than death, so forgiveness is stronger than sin. That may be the hardest thing in the faith to believe. The empty tomb is as nothing compared to the fact that we are indeed forgiven. But think again of Peter. Peter denied Christ just as surely as Judas betrayed him. The difference is that Peter came back to receive his forgiveness. The tragedy of Judas is that he never did.

Easter proclaims that forgiveness is offered all of us exactly as it was Peter. Just think: All the rulers of the world are forgiven, and church people too—including the pastors and priests who frequently have God in their mouths, but not so frequently in their hearts. *All* are forgiven. What does that mean? It means that we are relieved not of the consequences of our sin but of the consequences of being sinners. It means we are no longer sinners, but forgiven sinners. It means that with the zeal of gratitude we too can become ten times the people we are. It means that instead of trying to prove ourselves endlessly, we can express ourselves as fearless, vulnerable, dedicated, joyous followers of our risen Lord.

And now perhaps we can deal with the empty tomb. St. Paul was the earliest New Testament writer, and it is clear that his resurrection faith, like the faith of the disciples, was not based on the negative argument of an empty many a miracle story in the Bible, it may be an expression of faith rather than a basis of faith.

Convinced by his appearances that Jesus was their living Lord, the disciples really had only one category in which to articulate this conviction, and that was the doctrine of the resurrection of the dead. To St. Paul, the events of the last days had been anticipated, and God, by a mighty act, had raised Jesus from the dead—in a spiritual body. In Paul's writings, the living Christ and the Holy Spirit are never clearly differentiated, so that when he says, "Not I, but Christ who dwells within me," he is talking about the same Holy Spirit that you and I can experience in our own lives. I myself believe passionately in the resurrection of Jesus Christ, because in my own life I have experienced Christ not as a memory, but as a presence. So today on Easter we gather not, as it were, to close the show with the tune "Thanks for the Memory," but rather to reopen the show because "Jesus Christ is risen today."

There remains only to say a word about the final consequence Paul draws from the resurrection. "If . . . you are still in your sins . . . then those also who have died . . . have perished" (1 Cor. 15:17–18). What then are we to say of those who have died, and how are we to anticipate our own death?

The Bible is at pains to point out that life ends: "All flesh is grass" (Isa. 40:6). But St. Paul insists that "neither death, nor life . . . will be able to separate us from the love of God" (Rom. 8:38–39), that "whether we live or whether we die, we are the Lord's" (Rom. 14:8). If death, then, is no threat to our relationship to God; if, in the words of the Easter hymn, "made like him like him we rise, ours the cross, the grave, the skies"—then death should be no threat at all. If we don't know what is beyond the grave, we do know *who* is beyond the grave, and Christ resurrected links the two worlds, telling us we really live only in one. If God's love is immortal, then life is eternal, and death is a horizon, and a horizon is nothing save the limit of our sight. Can we not then also proclaim with St. Paul's wonderful freedom,

> Now this I say, brethren, that flesh and blood cannot inherit the kingdom of God; neither

doth corruption inherit incorruption. . . . For this corruptible must put on incorruption, and this mortal must put on immortality. So when this corruptible shall have put on incorruption, and this mortal shall have put on immortality, then shall be brought to pass the saying that is written, Death is swallowed up in victory. O death, where is thy sting? O grave, where is thy victory? . . . Thanks be to God, which giveth us the victory through our Lord Jesus Christ (1Cor. 15:50–57).

So sisters and brothers, what are we going to do on this blustery, glorious Easter Day? God has done God's part: resurrection has overcome crucifixion; forgiveness, sin; our departed loved

You report that just ahead for you are final exams and immediately thereafter the voter registration drive. Clearly idleness is not going to be your problem.

So here's what I propose. We've had the continuing correspondence you initiated last fall and which I've enjoyed enormously. As an academic year is no small stretch of time, and length is never the most important dimension in life, I suggest we continue to stay in touch, but in looser touch. My thought is that, for the summer at least, you write when you feel like it, and I, with more time, shall reply promptly, trying to pontificate and fulminate just a little bit less.

What do you say? Does this strike you as a suitable arrangement? You have said more than once that I have been a good teacher, but in my experience it is only when the student is ready that the teacher appears. Let me tell you, however, what teaching you has taught me.

I didn't realize I was quite so "worldly." By that I don't mean the shallow kind of this-worldliness in which we are "distracted from distraction by distraction." I mean a profound and robust commitment to the world God made and we live in. The afterlife I leave to God, who is merciful and far too busy for impertinent questions from me. I may want to know more, but I don't need to. "One world at a time"—that's my feeling and that's more than enough given the present anguish that engulfs it.

I share the view of Albert Camus that "there

is in this world beauty and there are the humiliated, and we must strive, hard as it is, not to be unfaithful, neither to the one nor to the other."

If as I suspect, Tom, you are a bit like me, then the more deeply you live in the world, the more you will live into the answers, and the more you will learn to believe.

I await your answer to my proposal. Still I cannot wait to tell you once again how much I love your fiery heart, the way you wear your learning lightly, and the delight you take simply in being alive on this earth. You are on your way to fulfilling the calling of every human being, which is to live a life worth the retelling of it—and, in your case, so much so that in Isaiah's words, "all the trees of the field shall clap their hands."

Emily Dickinson once more:

> That Love is all there is,
>
> Is all we know of Love.

Love,

Bill